MW01152571

Not A Purse

Written by Stephanie Dreyer
Illustrated by Jack Veda

NOT A PURSE By Stephanie Dreyer
ISBN 978-0-9861060-3-3

© 2018 by Stephanie Dreyer

All rights reserved. No part of this book may be used or reproduced in any matter whatsoever without the written permission of Stephanie Dreyer.

Book design and illustrations by Jack Veda

FIRST EDITION

For Mama Cow, who inspired my vegan journey,
and all animals everywhere.

Foreword

As a passionate animal activist, my love for our furry friends runs deep.

In *Not A Nugget*, Stephanie challenges us to see animals as friends, not food. She opens our eyes to the humanity of our animal pals and reminds us of the many ways we are similar to each other.

In her follow up book, *Not A Purse*, Stephanie takes families on a wonderful new adventure with the fuzzy critters we love, showing us all the ways animals are worn as clothing or beauty products, and used as home goods.

Her fun facts and beautiful illustrations are an enlightening look at the loveable, precious creatures who are exploited and harmed in the name of fashion, style and beauty.

I absolutely love this super-important book and know it will find a special place in your hearts, and in those you love.

- Kris Carr, New York Times best-selling author

Not a purse.

Did you know that cows know their names just like we do?

They can recognize their name when called.

Not a coat.

Did you know that minks like
to climb trees just like you?

Minks are skilled tree climbers,
able to jump from tree to tree.

Not a pillow.

Did you know that geese eat the same snacks that we do?

Geese love blueberries and eat other berries, nuts, and seeds too.

Not shampoo.

Did you know that pigs are great swimmers?

To cool down when it's hot,
pigs prefer water to mud and love to take a dip in the pool!

Not a hat.

Did you know that foxes love to play just like you?

Foxes especially love golf balls, which they swipe from golf courses!

Not a rug.

Did you know that zebras have "fingerprints" just like we do?

Instead of patterns on their fingers, zebras have stripes on their bodies that are unique to each animal, just as our fingerprints are one-of-a-kind to each of us.

Not a scarf.

Did you know that goats are great pals to have around?

Goats keep each other company on the farm
and are also great companions to their other
animal friends, such as cows, horses, and chickens.

Not a belt.

Did you know that ostriches love to take baths?

Ostriches love to be in water,
and frequently wash themselves in it.

Not a necklace.

Did you know that elephants hug each other just like we do?

Instead of using arms, elephants wrap their trunks together to greet each other and show affection.

Not a sweater.

Did you know that rabbits can see better than we can?

Rabbits have nearly 360° vision. They can see everything behind them with only a small blind spot in front of their nose.

Not a pair of boots.

Did you know that crocodiles cry just like you and I?

Crocodiles shed tears when they eat because they swallow too much air. This forces their tear glands to flow.

Not perfume.

Did you know that whales can recognize
each other's voices just like we can?

On diving trips, whales keep in touch with each
other using long-distance click sounds. Even if two
whales repeat the same pattern, faraway friends can
tell each other apart by each whale's unique sound.

Not a pair of gloves.

Did you know that sheep feel happy and sad just like you do?

Sheep share how they are feeling by their
facial expressions and the position of their ears.

Animals are our friends,

not clothing, beauty products, or home goods.

Other Fun Facts About Our Friends:

Sheep have very good memories. They can remember at least 50 individual sheep and humans for years.

Foxes have incredible hearing. Some foxes can hear a watch ticking 40 yards away!

Sperm whales are world class divers, able to descend to depths of over 3,280 feet and can go 90 minutes between breaths.

Elephants can swim, using their trunk to breathe like a snorkel in deep water.

Geese are loyal partners who mate for life. They produce two to six eggs each year.

Crocodiles are very strong swimmers. They have been spotted far out at sea.

Sheep are known to self-medicate when they are sick. When ill, they will eat specific plants that can cure them.

What else can we buy?

Instead of leather, suede, and other animal skins, buy clothing and products with faux versions of these materials that do not harm animals.

Instead of down (goose) feathers, buy products stuffed with man-made fibers or natural fillings such as kapok.

Instead of wool, mohair, or angora clothing, buy synthetic fabrics that don't come from an animal.

Instead of beauty products with keratin, biotin, amino and fatty acids, purchase cosmetics that use vegetable derived sources of ingredients.

Author's Note:

Leather and suede are materials made from animal skins such as cows, pigs, and other animals. Clothing is made from wool (sheep), mohair (goat), angora (rabbit), and cashmere (goat).

Many hygiene and beauty products are made of pig and other animals. Fatty acids extracted from the bone fat of pigs are used in shampoos and conditioners. These acids can also be found in body lotions, cosmetics, and anti-wrinkle creams.

Ivory from elephant tusks is used to make decorative objects, such as art, statues, ornaments, hair accessories, and jewelry. Although international trade of elephant ivory has been banned, elephant tusks are still used all over the world, especially in Asia.

Ambergris is a growth found in whale intestines and is used in making perfumes.

38466888R00024

Made in the USA
Columbia, SC
05 December 2018